Parent
Involvement
IS NON-NEGOTIABLE

Parent
Involvement
IS NON-NEGOTIABLE

Ronnie Phillips

Outskirts Press, Inc.
Denver, Colorado

Parent Involvement is Non-Negotiable
All Rights Reserved.
Copyright © 2009 Ronnie Phillips
v2.0 r1.2

Outskirts Press, Inc.
http://www.outskirtspress.com

ISBN: 978-1-4327-4328-4

Outskirts Press and the "OP" logo are trademarks belonging to Outskirts Press, Inc.

PRINTED IN THE UNITED STATES OF AMERICA

Table of Contents

Introduction

This book was created to assist parents with day-to-day strategies needed to develop educationally successful elementary-age children. Parents can follow these strategies at home. These methods have been proven successful by parents and educators.

I have spent thirty years in education at the elementary, middle, high, and adult levels. I have observed thousands of successful students and talked with thousands of parents. My successful experiences as an educator have enabled me to draw successful strategies from hundreds of successful parents and educators. Parents can use these techniques at home to help support their children.

Even though all subjects are important, we have included a number of strategies on how to become successful at the three R's (reading, writing, and arithmetic). In addition to the three R's, I have added additional characteristics of successful children and how parents can support them and meet their needs. Parents who follow these guidelines will prove successful in educating their children.

All parents would like their children to grow up to lead productive lives. Parents should realize that most successful children who have productive lives usually point to parental involvement as the biggest reason for their success. Since parents are often not "formally" taught how to raise educationally successful children, this book can help parents with proven guidelines.

Many parents learn how to raise successful children by mirroring the way their parents raised them. Some parents collaborate with other parents and gather useful information. Some parents leave everything up to the school and expect the school to provide their children with all the skills necessary for success.

Current studies indicate that when parents are involved in their children's education, children learn better, earn higher grades, and are more than likely to attend college. Some children are fortunate enough to have an outstanding teacher who motivates them to be an independent learner. As parents, we can't wait for something positive to happen to our children. We must make it happen. So utilize this book and any other information available to assist you with educating your children successfully.

All areas of education are important, but research states that reading is the best indicator of success. Parents should view successful reading skills as the strong yardstick for measuring educational growth.

Children should attend an elementary school that sets high standards for their students. Parents and elementary schools establish the foundation for future educational experiences. Parents must support the schools' activities by keeping their children focused on education at home. There are many avenues to making this possible. Many are covered in this book. Elementary-school teachers leave lasting impressions on students, so it is important that those experiences are positive and wholesome. Choosing a good elementary school as well as good teachers is a must, and parents should be intrinsically involved in that process.

The information in this book is very valuable for parents and children. We are also in need of a Higher Power to give us directions in raising productive children. Be sure to include prayer before making decisions concerning children, and you won't go wrong

Acknowledgements

This book is dedicated to my family, my deceased father Clyde, my mother Inez, my brothers Lamar and Maurice, and my sisters Brenda and Loretta. Your support has always been an inspiration to me. I truly appreciate the many times you have helped to develop me into the person I am today. God couldn't have placed me into a better family. I hope I have in some way lived up to some of your expectations.

Many thanks also go to my deceased uncle Jack and my living uncle William and aunt Marsh-Lee and deceased aunt Babe-Ruth. You have always provided wisdom throughout my life. Sometimes I had to endure long speeches from you, but the wisdom that came out of those speeches was truly appreciated. A special tribute to my deceased grandmother and grandfather Manuel who demonstrated the importance of hard work throughout their lives and who passed those same traits down to my father, uncles, and aunts.

I am particularly grateful to my wife Lisa for keeping me focused and providing the refinement that was needed in my life. You have truly provided the love, support, and encouragement that I needed. Also, thank you for delivering our children Ronnie and Jasmine. They are truly what makes our family complete. I am thankful that we are keeping our family tradition going and building a strong future for our offspring. We must always remember how important our family is and continue to support them in every way possible.

Our family is important, but we must never forget that God is the one who has provided the many blessings we have, and the closer we get to Him, the stronger our family will be. So I am giving a special thanks to God for keeping our family together and providing the wisdom needed to survive in this world.

A special thanks to Josephine Belford and Jacqueline Solomon for providing technical support in a time of need. A true friend is someone who steps up in a time of need, and both of you did, so, thank you.

Lastly, special thanks goes to all of the many students that I have had the pleasure to learn from in my many years in the educational arena. It is you who have given me the inspiration to work on this project. The many hours I have observed, counseled, disciplined, and listened to you has given me a thorough understanding of what it takes to be successful in education and in life. I hope I have given you some kind of knowledge that has helped you in your education and/or life. Thank you and keep up the good work!

Choosing An Elementary School

1

The educational choices parents make at home with children are very important to the overall educational process. Equally important is the school that children attend. Choosing a good school is one of the most important and difficult decisions a parent will make. Elementary schools provide the foundation for educating children. This chapter will provide parents with valuable information to help make an informed choice when selecting an elementary school for their children.

Where the family lives can play a big role in determining what school the children will attend. However, in today's society, parents have some leeway in choosing what elementary school children attend. Parents are no longer obligated to send children to the public school in their neighborhood.

Because of the variety of new schools available, parents now have choices. The larger cities have more choices, be it public, private, or charter. The size of the city has a lot to do with what kind of educational choices are available in that area. The larger the city, naturally, the more choices are available for children. Families in suburban areas also have many choices, but children may have to travel further to attend some schools.

Parents should do a thorough investigation before making a decision as to what school to send their children. Parents should make sure to choose a school that best fits the children's needs and the expectations of parents.

In making a decision, one of the most important factors is: what does the school have to offer the children? As parents do research, they will find that some schools provide strong discipline,with uniforms and strong student code of conduct policies. Other schools provide strong technology curriculums, and some even require computers for every student. And others provide a curriculum for students who are interested in the arts. Parents need to become knowledgeable about different schools in their neighborhood. The next section describes a few of the many theme schools available throughout our country.

Schools of Choice

Before making a decision as important as what elementary school the children will attend, parents should become familiar with the many kinds of schools available. Experts in the education field agree that no one type of school is best for all children. A variety of educational approaches on how to educate children have been developed. Parents need to do their research and become familiar with the variety of schools in order to make a good decision about where to enroll their children. This section will provide a list of several kinds of schools with a brief summary of their focus.

- Charter Schools: These schools are run independently of school districts, but within the public school boundaries. These schools were created to provide choices for parents. They are supposed to offer new and innovative ways to raise student achievement without the normal restrictions found in public school districts.

- Fine Arts Schools: These schools require students to concentrate on the arts. Students can expect to be involved in drama, music, and plays. Students must audition and submit an application for admission.

- Foreign Language Schools: Students in these schools are required to take several foreign languages throughout their elementary career. Generally, children from all cultures are enrolled in these schools. Children not only have an opportunity to learn several languages, but they also learn about different cultures. An application is required for admission.

- Honor Schools: These schools focus on all higher level academics. Some of these schools require students to work at a faster pace than regular elementary schools. Students are usually required to take entrance exam to be admitted into these schools.

- Magnet Schools: These schools offer a special curriculum capable of attracting a substantial number of students from different racial backgrounds. They were developed to facilitate voluntary desegregation. Most magnet programs focus on academics (mathematics, natural science, and social science), or they may focus on technical/vocational/agricultural education.

- Montessori Schools: These schools emphasize self-directed activities on the part of the child and clinical observations on the part of the teacher. This approach stresses the importance of adapting the child's learning environment to his/her development level.

▪ Private Schools: Independent schools that charge a fee to attend. Classes are generally smaller and students almost always wear uniforms.

▪ Progressive Schools: These schools are strongly influenced by what the children are interested in and are children-centered and not adult-driven. The curriculum is more flexible and influenced by student interest. Progressive education programs often include the community resources and encourage service-learning projects.

▪ Neighborhood Public Schools: These are schools that are located in the neighborhood in which you live. Students are accepted from within a particular boundary. Some of these schools will have a special focus.

▪ Smaller Schools: These schools are small in population and have special grants to keep the size of school small. The curriculum may vary. The big push is to keep the school small and with more nurturing, which should lead to an outstanding education.

▪ Waldorf Schools: These schools provide an education that mirrors the basic stages of a child's development from childhood to adulthood.

School Investigation

When investigating a school, parents need to make sure they know what characteristics to look for. It makes no sense to conduct an investigation of elementary schools if parents don't know what they are looking for. This section will provide parents with some important information that can be useful when identifying what a good elementary school looks like. Some of the characteristics of a high achieving school, which will be discussed in chapter two are: school test scores, school curriculum, parental involvement, school leadership, school uniforms, school discipline, and after-school programs.

Time should be spent researching as much information about elementary schools as possible before actually going out and talking to people about the school. This book, and additional information, can be located online, which describes what good elementary schools have in common. Once a list of qualities for a good elementary school has been developed, parents can start identifying schools in their city that meet those qualifications.

Parent should remember that part of the investigation includes going to the schools to see how they run, attending parent meetings, reviewing test scores, talking to people who work in the school or live in the school community. Also, obtaining a copy of the rules and regulations of the school is important. As with any major decision a parent makes, after the investigation is completed, add up the pluses and minuses and make an informed decision.

Characteristics of Effective Schools

2

Test Scores

One of the most important factors used to determine the success of a school is its standardized test results. Standardized tests are a good indicator of how the entire school is achieving academically. They can also be used to determine if the teaching staff is doing a good job preparing students for standardized tests. These tests are recommended by the local, state, or federal government. High-achieving schools generally have high test scores.

Students from all over the state or country take some form of standardized tests throughout their educational experience. Whichever test the school uses, it is used to gauge where their children's educational aptitude is for each subject area. The results are a comparison to other students throughout the state and country. Children will be compared to other children using standardized tests from elementary school through college.

As part of the investigation, the parents should ask the school for a copy of the last three years of test results. Schools are glad to share test scores if results are good. The results will give parents more of a history of how the school has performed in the past. Also, most public schools' test scores can be found on that state's Web site. Tests are important, but should not be the only tool used to evaluate a good school. Parents should also keep in mind that some standardized tests contain such extremely high standards that the entire state has difficulty scoring well.

Parents should compare test scores from their top three school choices and use the test results to rate the top achieving schools. Parents should also realize that the English/language arts and mathematics test scores are probably most important during the elementary school years. If the mathematics and English/language arts scores are high, it means the school is probably doing a good job of developing a solid foundation for the students in their building.

Academic Approach/Curriculum

Test results are important in evaluating the school, but equally as important is understanding the curriculum utilized to educate the students. It is very important to know if the school is using the state-required curriculum or if the school is using its own curriculum. If the school is using the state curriculum and the teachers are doing a good job of teaching the state curriculum, when children take the state standardized tests, the results should be good.

Most public school districts follow the state curriculum. If the school is not following the state curriculum, the parents should be cautious. Parents need to acquire more information about the school to know what kind of curriculum is being used and if that curriculum is in alignment with the state standards. Also, parents will need to know if that curriculum has a successful proven track record and where the parent can get more information about that curriculum.

With the variety of schools available, if parents aren't careful, their children will end up in a school that is not meeting the academic standards for their age groups. Some schools are new and haven't had a chance to develop a strong curriculum, and if children are enrolled, they run the risk of missing vital instructions. These elementary school years are too important to have gaps in a child's education, so parents should look for the best available educational opportunity in their city.

Parental Involvement

Parental involvement is probably the most important characteristic of successful schools. The schools that have strong parental participation tend to be high-achieving schools.

Schools that allow parents to come in the building and assist with different activities throughout the school year are demonstrating a team approach to education. This can lead to a number of positive things happening for the school. Parents may have affiliations with community organizations that could lead to advantages for the school. These schools normally have lots of fundraisers from the parent organization and parents volunteer in the school throughout the day and after school.

These schools also have an open-door policy for parents. Parents can come up to the school at any time and can check on children while in class. Children become used to adults being in their building, which generally promotes better behavior for children. The staff generally go the extra mile to help develop positive relationships with parents. This kind of participation should be high on the list of requirements for an effective elementary school.

Because of the importance of parental involvement, some schools provide a parent center for parents. This room is usually equipped with a computer, books, and a telephone for parents to use. The bigger the room, the more activities the parent group can offer. This is a clear indication of how the school feels about the parents.

The successful schools generally have a strong PTA or parent organization. The PTA is an intricate part of the school, and all major school decisions have some input from the PTA. The PTA regularly meets with the principal to brainstorm ways to help improve the school.

Before making a decision about the school, the parents should attend a parent meeting at the school and ask questions about: What kind of relationship do the parents have with the principal and the teachers? What are the positive and negative features about the school? Parents can ask additional questions at the meeting that may directly impact their children. This should supply parents with solid information to form a parent's perspective.

School Leadership

When a parent is choosing a school, one of the most important characteristics of the school is who is in charge of the building. Ideally, the principal has full control of the building and when a parent visits, the school is running in an orderly fashion. If parents enter a building and notice the staff are not working and children are allowed to do whatever they please without adult supervision, this school may have some leadership problems. This might not be the best school for your children. There are various leadership styles which parents should be aware of in order to make an intelligent decision about which school to enroll their children at. The two styles that are most prevalent in school leadership are authoritarian and participative.

Authoritarian

Parents should find out as much information as possible about the leadership style of the principal before making a decision on a school. The principal will be the person who will set the tone or influence the climate of the building. Some principals make every decision in the building, which may or may not lead to good student success in that building. This kind of principal is on every committee, and he/she is in charge of all meetings. Generally, his/her school is orderly because of the fear of the principal.

Everyone in the building will know their role in the school, because the principal will dictate all roles. This kind of principal will make sure students and staff understand and follow the disciplinary procedures of the building. The staff that works under this kind of leader must be an obedient soldier to tolerate that style.

In these schools, the staff or parents may or may not feel a part of the school, because the principal dictates the operation of everything. The intelligence and skills of the staff are not fully utilized because of the final decisions made by the principal. Sometimes tension is high in these buildings. This kind of leadership style can lead to a lack of "buy-in" from the staff and parents.

When looking at this kind of leadership style, ask yourself, will my children learn in this kind of environment? Is the staff giving 100 percent to the students? Is school achievement high? Is this a good school for children?

Participative

On the other hand, principals who allow and encourage input from their staff and parents will have more "buy-in" from all parties. This kind of principal will make most decisions based on what the majority decides. These principals will generally have an open-door policy for students, staff, and parents. He/she will have a representative on all committees, but he will not serve on all committees. Because of the mutual respect that exists, committees will still solicit the principal's opinion for all major decisions.

This kind of principal will know how to utilize his or her staff and get the most productivity from them. Each staff member feels empowered to make decisions. Every staff member knows their role because they helped develop them with the support of the principal.

These schools are generally positive and everyone believes the entire school is working toward educating the children in that building. These schools will have the staff enrolling their own children in that school, because the staff will trust the entire staff, and they have first-hand knowledge of the good work being done in the building. Parents participate willingly in school activities. These principals encourage the staff and parents to be involved in the entire school operation.

The participative leadership style has a positive effect on the students in the building. Generally, students' discipline problems are fewer, because students respect an administration that seems concerned about them. The positive atmosphere motivates the students to perform to the best of their ability, which eliminates much of the negative behaviors. Students will be made aware of all policies and procedures. Students will be encouraged to form clubs and organizations and participate in the overall school functions.

Parents must decide which leadership style will work best for their children.

Uniforms

There has been much debate as to whether school uniforms should be required for school-age children or if children should be allowed to have individual choices on what they wear. This is something that parents will have to decide. Research has shown a clear perception of less violence in schools where children wear uniforms. The parents and community believe that less focus on fashion will help increase students' achievement in school. There is no evidence to support that charge, but schools enforcing uniform policies seem to have a calmer school climate and children are not preoccupied with clothing.

In 2000, Lands' End, the clothing retailer, in partnership with the National Association of Elementary School Principals, commissioned a telephone survey of principals that netted 755 responses. According to the principals surveyed, school-uniform policies had a positive effect on the following areas: image in the community (84 percent of principals surveyed agreed); classroom discipline (79 percent agreed); peer pressure (76 percent agreed); school spirit (72 percent agreed); concentration on schoolwork (67 percent agreed); and school safety (62 percent agreed) (NAESP 2000).

Another important benefit for parents is the cost of the uniforms. Uniforms are not expensive and are easy to find. The savings can be directed into other educational areas for children.

From a personal experience as a principal, our policy had the following impact: school uniforms had a very positive impact on the students, violence decreased, and students' behavior seemed to be better after school uniforms were instituted. Student achievement also increased. More incentives to adhere to the uniform policy created a positive attitude from students throughout the school year. Schools with uniforms should have other positive programs in place as well to help increase student achievement.

School Discipline

Parents should pay careful attention as to what kind of discipline procedures are being administered in the school. It is better to find out before enrolling children into a school rather than face the consequences of the school procedures later.

Schools, school districts, and teachers have different methods of disciplining students, and parents have the right to know what those methods are. Some school districts have a strict code of conduct for students and each school is required to follow it. Other districts allow each school to develop its own classroom discipline procedures. Further, some schools allow teachers to develop their own discipline procedures.

Whatever method the schools uses, the procedures should be known to all parents and the school should set up a time to discuss the procedures with the parents and students. The successful discipline policies should include contacting the parents early in the discipline process. Children have a tendency to behave better when there's a consequence of a parental notification.

Once the school is selected, the parents should remember to be supportive of the discipline procedures of the school. Whatever discipline the children receive at school the parents should reinforce at home. Bad behavior will change more quickly if the children know the parents will support whatever discipline procedures are administered at school.

Most parents realize that elementary children are in need of firm, but fair discipline at school and at home. The school's discipline procedures should not be one-sided, where children are punished all the time. The key to a good discipline program is for children to know what is expected of them and what the consequences are if rules are violated.

After-School and Summer-School Programs

Equally as important as choosing an elementary school is choosing an after-school or summer-school program for children. After-school and summer programs will assist with the overall development of children. Children will spend six to seven hours a day in school for approximately nine months out of the year. The remaining time of the day and year must be used constructively to guarantee success for children. In order to maximize that extra time, children need to learn life skills in non classroom settings. Most effective after-school and summer-school programs are structured, but they do allow children the time to have freedom to explore and become creative.

There are several after-school programs in and around major cities in our country. The question might be what program is best suited for our children? Other questions might be what is the focus of the after-school or summer program? Does the program have good supervision? Is the program well organized?

When parents make a decision to put children in an after-school program, they should know what they want to gain from the program. The parents should know if they are looking for tutorial help. The program should not be set up in a classroom setting, because the program will run the risk of having the children shut down because of being tired from a whole day of instruction before the after-school program even begins.

If parents are looking for a place to have children learn how to play an instrument, they should be willing to purchase an instrument for practice. Parents should also know if the children are in need of physical activities. If so, placing the children in an organized sports program would be a possibility. If parents choose a sports program, they should make sure the program stresses learning the basics and not "winning at all cost." Or perhaps you are looking for some place where your children can play and socialize with other children.

The best way to begin looking for after-school programs is to talk to the school personnel and investigate what they have to offer. Also, neighborhood recreation centers, Boys Club, and the YMCA should have a directory of after-school and summer programs. Spend some time talking to parents whose children participated in local after-school programs. Once you have identified a program, be sure to check out how safe the program is, what kind of supervision is in place, how affordable it is, and if it fit into your schedule. Monitor the program after the children have begun to participate to see if it delivers what it promised.

We have had both of our children in summer programs throughout their lives. My son has been involved in organized sports as well as summer camps. The exposure he received was very valuable for his athletic and social development. By participating in after-school programs, he learned how to play the piano as well as participated in various creative activities. These activities led to a lot of social growth throughout the year.

My daughter participated in summer programs that were more geared toward academic enrichment, which I believe has led to her becoming more academically motivated. She did participate in some sports activities throughout the summer, but her main focus was academic enrichment, which was more of a need for her at that time in her life.

We were able to find summer programs that were interesting and educationally helpful for her. Some of her programs involved building objects such as cars, planes, and robotics. With the interest the summer and Saturday programs created, her academic motivation improved and she began to take school very seriously. Her grades improved, and she earned several 4.0 GPAs in school.

I can't give summer programs all the credit, because as parents, we spent a lot of time having her read as many books as possible, as well as utilizing other strategies to improve her grades. Quality time does pay off.

Summer is also a good time to develop some of the nonacademic subjects such as: music, art, and sports. Children can participate in church camps, dance programs, or just travel with parents. All summer enrichment programs can be beneficial for children, but be sure children have some input about their preferences during the summer. However, parents should make sure some kind of educational benefits will be derived from the summer programs.

Creativity is important at the elementary-school age, and summer is a time when children can develop their creativity. It helps to find those programs where the staff incorporates creativity in their programs. These programs generally have staff who work with children on a regular basis. In these programs, children produce some kind of project before the end of the summer. These classes are project-based.

Keep whatever project your children produce. This may come in handy at a later date. Children's success is important to help keep them motivated.

Parents should recognize what subject area the children are having trouble with and find a summer program that has academic improvement in that area as the outcome. Try to find a program that uses some kind of creative method to reach the children. This kind of program may spark the interest of the children and help improve academic weaknesses. For example, some summer programs in engineering encourage children to design, build, or create projects with other students. This program could improve math, science, and reading skills.

Another important factor about these programs is the fact that they have children engaged with other children. Children generally like to look good around their peers, which could be a motivating force for them. This may help them try harder, and improving academics may be the end result.

What Parents Can Do
To Develop Successful Children

3

Raising children is a difficult job for parents. Throughout their elementary-school years, children are influenced by numerous people. Influences can be both negative and positive. Adults and peers are the biggest influence in the development of children's attitudes toward life. Parents, teachers, and peers are all key people in children's development. The importance of having strong positive people around children can not be stressed enough.

When parents are making decisions for their children, the children with whom they socialize should be a top priority. Remember the old saying that goes, "You can pay me now, or you can pay me later." If children are allowed to hang out with children who do not have structure at home and are constantly in trouble, what do you think is most likely to happen to them? Children sometimes get so close to their peers, that can be frightening. Peers can influence friends to do the types of things that parents might not approve. The solution is to help select children's peers from day one and pray!!

This is one of those situations when the parent needs to step up and be a parent. Children are sometimes too young to know what is best for them. Children should not be allowed to develop any serious friendship unless parents approve of the person and the family. This approval includes knowing who the parents are and what kind of household they keep. Are the children polite and do they have manners? Most importantly, is education important in their home? Are there books in their home? The answer to these questions can help parents make a sound decision when choosing peers.

This chapter has excellent strategies to assist parents in raising successful children. Parents must have a positive and caring attitude themselves in order to help their children. Parents who are constantly hollering and fussing at their children are doing an injustice to the development of those children. Parents are, in a sense, stunting the growth of the children by engaging in this constant, negative behavior.

Numerous studies have been done that indicate what children are exposed to during the early years will help shape who they become in the later years. This means parents need to provide as many positive situations as possible for their children, and hopefully, the children will lead a normal and productive life. Surrounding children with positive adults and peers who have some of the same values as the parents can assist parents with shaping the children into the kind of person parents deem productive.

When children begin to attend school, parents should choose the school they will attend, but more importantly, parents should be involved in the school. Parents should investigate all teachers that will be teaching their children. Parents should try to direct their children to the more challenging teachers who seem to be fair with their students. If you have to change schools to find excellent teachers, I suggest you do so. Remember that children will be in school about seven hours a day, so whoever provides instruction to them is very important.

When our son was going into the first grade, we knew of a first-grade teacher at another school who was an excellent reading teacher. She had developed a special phonics program for all of her students. As a result, all of the older children who had previously been in her class were excellent readers. I knew she was the right teacher for my son. Being in her class would improve our son's reading skills, and it did.

I enrolled my son in that school so he could benefit from her instruction, even though the school was not in our neighborhood. Sometimes you have to make sacrifices for your children. Our son became an excellent reader throughout his career thanks to his first-grade teacher.

His second-grade teacher was equally as good at teaching math. In that second-grade class, the students were taught multiplication, division, addition, subtraction, and square roots. His teacher also taught the class how to do mental math. Most of those students went on to become excellent math students. Teachers play an extremely important role in the children's educational process.

Success

In order for children to be successful, parents need to think about what is considered successful. What would "successful" children look like? What is it that parents want for their children? What is it that children want? How do you get there? Make a list of the characteristics you would prefer in your children.

Some parents think successful children are children who get all A's in class. Some parents want their children to excel in sports. Some parents would like to see their children successful in music. Others are happy because children are not in trouble and are passing their classes. Lastly, some parents want well-adjusted children who respect adults.

Whatever the parents' idea of a successful child, everything begins by parents believing in the children and supporting them throughout their life. Children need to know that their parents are in their corner and will always support them whatever career choices they make. Parents need to realize they can positively influence children's choices in life if they supply all the right ingredients and information necessary for their success. This chapter will assist parents in identifying what characteristics should be developed in successful children.

This section will also supply parents with a number of strategies that can be implemented at home and are directly linked to successful children. Children who follow the lead of their parents with the guidelines presented will be successful in school as well as life. Additional items could be added, but the guidelines in this book are a start for parents to begin to develop successful children.

How to Organize Home for Success

Thomas is a nine-year-old, and he lives in a house that is very neat and well kept. He has been engaged in household routines since the age of four. He keeps his room clean and takes out the garbage every day. He has space in his home designated for his schoolwork as well as a schedule for all of his activities. Thomas is well organized and is successful at school. His parents have very high expectations for him, and he has lived up to most of their expectations as of this date.

Mary is an eight-year-old, and she lives in a household where the parents don't believe in requiring their children to do much work around the house. They believe children should play and be kids. There is not a lot of structure in this household in terms of when and where to do homework and what time to go to sleep at night. Mary has a lot of toys, but doesn't spend a lot of time keeping toys off the floor of her bedroom. She doesn't really work at being a good student. She barely has passing grades, and that is good enough for her parents. Her parents believe she will mature as she grows older and her grades will improve. Mary's parents were not good students when they were in school.

In which home would most parents choose for their children to be raised? Being organized at home is another one of the keys to success. Children being raised in a positive, structured environment have a much better chance of being successful and being productive in life. This chapter will show how being organized at home and teaching children how to be organized can contribute to success.

When I was growing up, my parents required me to do work around the house, keep my bedroom clean, and perform whatever other chores were needed. As a little boy, I helped my father paint the exterior of the house, wash dishes for a week at a time, cut the grass, take out the garbage, and clean my bedroom on a regular schedule. Also, I was required to do my homework every night. That structure my parents provided for me gave me the foundation to be successful in life.

Parents need to structure their children's life as early as possible for future successes. Being organized doesn't mean that children can't be children and play and do many of the things children do. But it does mean parents need to be involved in important decisions made concerning their children's day-to-day experiences.

Foundations laid by my parents gave me the chance to become successful. Successful habits were developed because my parents had high expectations. Good habits that are developed at a young age can carry children a long way. Some simple habits that should be present in all homes are: a set time to eat dinner each day, a set time to do homework each day, a set time to go to bed, a set time to get up each morning, and a set time to do chores, to name only a few.

As you can see, the examples we set for our children early on will determine how they live their lives. As children grow older, one of their major examples will come from the parents' home. In order for children to be organized, parents must set the first positive example.

Parents should know that there may be a direct relationship between a clean, well organized home and how much education and financial success children will achieve. Parents should always be looking for every advantage for their children, and if developing successful children is as simple as keeping a clean and orderly home, all of our homes should be clean. But, by no means am I saying that children must come from an organized, clean home in order to be successful. Children can learn in any environment, but an organized environment is more conducive to success.

One way to get started on this task is to throw out all possessions in your home that are no longer useful. Make room for an educational environment that is conducive to success. Some parents give their used clothing and shoes to the Salvation Army. Throw out all unusable home items that are in the way and just collecting dust. Whatever it takes to make room for an organized home, parents should make that determination. Once room is available in their home, parents should plan on organizing a home that fosters success.

Parents should think about placing educational items throughout the house to keep children aware of how important education is. When parents purchase paintings that depict people from other countries, the children should be made aware of what country the people originate from and some additional basic information about the paintings. Remember, we are developing an educational environment for successful children and everything in the house can help.

One of the most important things in the house that enhances the educational environment is bookshelves and books. We can't seriously talk about educating our children and not have books in the house for them to read. How many times have parents been in someone's house and saw no books to read? That is a house that is not conducive to education. The kind of books is not important, but certain books should be placed on the bookshelves to support children's education. It is also very important to include educational books and tools for children, such as: dictionaries, encyclopedias, research books, globes, microscopes, telescopes, and calculators.

If the house is big enough to set aside a special room for educational tools, this would be very helpful for children and adults. This room should be well lit and have a large desk or table with a computer and printer that has access to the Internet. This would be a perfect place to have the bookshelves and numerous books. The room should be equipped with a telephone, fax, and scanner. This technology is necessary to keep up with the way we live in the twenty-first century. This room would allow children to do their research and complete school assignments from grades K–12 without leaving the house to do so. Parents should be prepared to assist their children from the comforts of their home. This is a twenty-first-century educational environment.

Once the educational environment is set, the children should be required to keep the room clean. The sole responsibility of keeping that room clean and orderly should be left up to them. This is a good time to develop responsibility with children. Parents should make sure their children know what the consequences will be for not keeping a clean room. Parents should decide what the consequences are, but make sure the penalty fits the crime. In other words, don't over punish children for not cleaning up the room.

In the bedroom, children should have bookshelves. The more books the better. When books are taken off the shelf for use, children should be taught to put them back in their place. This is part of teaching children how to be organized and neat.

Also, a desk with a light would be appropriate. This desk could be a quiet place for children to study. After placing the desk in the bedroom, parents should take time to explain how to keep the desk organized and clear of clutter. The key to having order in the children's bedroom is to keep everything neat. Parents must make frequent visits to their children's bedroom to check the status of cleanliness. Parents should remember that the house, bedroom, basement, etc., are all part of an educational environment.

Additional Home Strategies

The younger children's room can be educationally enhanced by placing alphabets on the walls of their bedroom. Place the letters high on the walls so children can see them every night. Alphabets on the wall can also help with the awareness of letters for the younger children. Children will become comfortable with seeing letters every day as reinforcement.

As the children grow older, the letters should be replaced with small three- and four-letter words. Each word placed on the wall should be a part of the child's vocabulary. Make sure the children know the meaning of every word on the wall and can place the word in a sentence. Reading those words will become easy for the children, and reading confidence will improve. At night, they may even dream about the words on the wall. The child's vocabulary will improve with this little technique. Some parents go straight to words and never use the alphabet technique. You be the judge, depending on your child's readiness.

The same techniques can be done with a math wall for children. Numbers and math computation problems can be placed on children's walls. Numbers from 1 to 50 on the wall could be very informative for children. Basic adding and subtraction problems are a good beginning. Children will see these numbers and problems every day before going to sleep.

These two techniques are a good start to developing an organized room that is conducive to learning. At an early age, children want to please their parents, so they will attempt to learn as much as possible. If children start life thinking about letters, words, and math problems, they will have a good jump start on their educational journey. What a wonderful way to start the child's educational awareness in the home.

Children who are starting to develop a vocabulary are in need of knowing the names of the various objects in their everyday lives. Labeling objects in the house is a good technique parents can use to increase younger children's vocabulary When children see the name of an object that is labeled, they will become familiar with the name of that object and their vocabulary will instantly increase. Once again, children should be a part of the labeling, cutting out of words, and placing them on objects throughout the house.

Use this time as a teaching moment and talk with children about each word being placed on the objects. These words will also become a part of the children's new vocabulary. If the children are not familiar with the words, put the words in sentences and explain the words to them. Some of these techniques may seem basic, but if the children develop these basic techniques at home, school will be more rewarding for them.

Another strategy to encourage reading would be to place reading material in each of the rooms in the house. Some of the rooms that might be included could be the bathroom, den, living room, kitchen, bedroom, and basement. Children who see reading material all over the house will be influenced by what is important to the parents. Parents are planting a seed, and it will grow over time.

The educational environment can be enhanced further by having parents display diplomas, college degrees, or other kinds of awards parents earned. Parents should also put together a scrapbook of certificates and pictures of successful events in children's and adults' lives. This is a good way to show what parents and children have accomplished in life. This can be encouragement for children to strive for awards.

Parents should pick a busy room in the house such as the basement or the den and place positive posters on the wall. Children will grow up with positive messages all through the house. In a house that strongly implies that education is of importance, children will start to value education. Once parents convince their children of the importance of education, the future journey will be easier. Self-motivated children are usually very successful in whatever they decide to do in life. These children do not wait for someone to tell them what to do; they do it on their own.

Another tool to enhance the educational environment is having a large calendar placed in a room to which everyone has easy access. This calendar should be used to place all important dates and events for the household. Children's important dates should be very special and parents should make sure their children's events are on that calendar and all appointment are kept. A good place for the calendar is the kitchen, because everyone uses that room daily.

In addition to the calendar, the children's report cards can be placed on the refrigerator where everyone can see them. If the grades are good, the children can't wait to show them off. If the grades are bad, the children will hesitate about placing report cards on the refrigerator. Once the parents have decided to place report cards on refrigerator, it should be done whatever the grades—good or bad. Hopefully, children will work hard to improve their grades when necessary.

Parents should work with children in creating a weekly schedule. Children can be involved in so many activities that a schedule is needed. Schedules are reminders to children and parents to make sure all activities are achieved. Schedules lend themselves to success. Knowing what to do, where to do it, and what time it should be done is part of an organized lifestyle. Parents should arrange their schedules with their children as the number-one priority.

Parents should also remember that some children will not conform to all of your requests. Some things you can demand, but remember the object is to get the job done. If children have success doing something another way, leave them alone. However, never compromise on organizational methods you think are absolutely necessary.

Another requirement that should be insisted upon by parents is assigning chores to children. Children should have chores around the house and not expect pay for them. Rewarding children sometimes for a specific accomplishment is okay, but this should not be overdone. Rewarding children for everything will cause problems later in life. Children must understand that their parents are providing all of their basic needs, and all they ask in return is that the children do their chores around the house and give 100 percent at school.

The television could be one of the most destructive tools in your house, if not utilized properly. There are a lot of very good educational programs on television, but most children don't view them. In order to help children stay on target with their education, you need to limit the amount of time children watch television and play games throughout the week. A general recommendation is to stop television viewing or playing games during the week. Children will have plenty of homework and extracurricular activities to keep them busy. The weekend can be used for television or Nintendo games. Once this rule is established in the house, the children will quickly adapt to it and parents will see more focus on school-related assignments.

Additional successful routines could include using the same time every day to study and complete homework. Children work better when they know what is expected of them each and every day. If Joe arrives home every day at 3:30 p.m. and at 4:00 p.m. starts his homework, there is no excuse as to what Joe is required to do every day at 4:00 p.m. The entire house will know what is expected of him, and they can respect his time as well. The schedule might include doing chores around the house at a certain time. Children should know what is expected of them, and as a parent, you will then have better control of the home.

Parental Involvement

When parents come home after spending a full day at work, sometimes the last thing they look forward to doing is active involvement with their children. It is very hard for parents, but the parents who do make that sacrifice will see the rewards in the success of their children. The old saying is true, "Wherever there are successful children, there are involved parents." If the family is truly what is important, whatever happens at your job will be put on a back burner when children are at stake. This is truly how parental involvement begins. When children go to school every day, they need to believe that their parents are going to be there for them when help is needed.

Once parents have made the commitment to be involved with their children, the school and teachers should be high on the list of participation. A very important task that can be started at home is to help children develop good feelings about their teachers and their school. Parents should constantly talk about how important teachers and school are to the success of everyone. Being successful in school leads to successful careers.

In order to show the children their parents mean business, they should meet with the children's teachers on a regular basis, and, if possible, spend time in the children's school, volunteering. Children have respect for parents who are in their building and are a part of the school. This helps the children feel more at ease and confident because of positive relationships the parents have developed with teachers and the school in general.

The involved parents should know what is going on with their children's school and at home. That includes making it a point to meet the principal. Whenever a situation arises where the parent needs to meet with the principal, it helps to already have a positive relationship. Parents who only meet with principals when there are problems with their children tend to be combative and not aware of the policies and procedures of the school. More often than not, the parent is not happy with the outcome of the meeting with the principal in this type of situation.

Parental involvement does stop with meeting the principal and the teacher. When parents get involved with other parents, they develop relationships that will benefit their children. This can be done in a number of ways. The first way is to have parents attend the school PTA or parent organization meeting. As a parent, you need to attend these meetings and get involved so you will know what is happening in the school. Even though school personnel will probably tell you they have the best school in America, schools are not perfect, but parents can help them improve. Whatever role a parent plays with the parent organization will be a plus for the school and their child's benefit.

Another way parents can get involved is through networking. Try to meet some of the other parents in your children's classes and develop some dialogue. Parents can assist each other with ways to support their children. Some parents may be aware of special programs or sports teams that may be beneficial to other parents. Parents may help each other with transportation to different events. Some parents may have had other children who have matriculated through that school and can share advice on which teachers they recommend. The sharing of information can be invaluable to the success of children.

Lastly, parental involvement should be a daily routine for parents with their children. Parents should make sure every day that children's needs are met. When children come home from school, parents should have a routine set for their children so that they will know when homework should be done, when household chores need to be done, who will take them to their extracurricular activities, how much television is appropriate, etc.

Parents should check all homework assignments to see if the children have completed the assignments and if they need help. When parents notice children are having difficulty in a subject, it is up to that parent to get help right away and not wait for the school to provide help. This is what true parental involvement is all about.

The parents who make sure their children go to school every day know who their children's teachers are, know their peers, help children with homework, require children to read, enroll children in educational enrichment programs outside of school, are involved in the school, and provide encouragement for their children. These parents are on their way to developing successful children.

Homework Strategies

If teachers were asked what is the most important way for parents to support teachers from home, the answer would probably be: make sure children do homework every night. Homework is something all parents should put a high priority on in their home.

When children come home from school each day, parents need to make the decision of when children should do their homework assignments. Some parents believe doing homework when children get home from school is appropriate, while others prefer to wait until later in the night to do homework. While this may not seem important, it is important for the children. The children's schedule will probably dictate what time to start homework.

Whatever time the child starts the homework assignments, parents should try to keep up with what the child is working on in school so they will be better prepared to assist the children, if needed. Some teachers will even give students some kind of course outline that will tell parents exactly what the class will be working on with specific information week by week of what will be covered.

Homework is a must for all successful children, and if a teacher is not assigning homework, the parent needs to meet with the teacher right away. If the parent can't resolve the problem with the teacher, the problem should be taken to one of the administrators in the building. One of the reasons homework is so important is that it will reinforce what the children have learned in school, which will help teachers cover more material and allow children to learn more.

The time spent on homework will increase from around twenty minutes during kindergarten to a couple of hours or more a night in high school.

Once parents know what material is being covered in school, parents can try to find other resources that will help their children better understand their studies. This can be done by having a computer at home with access to the Internet. Parents can assist their children to research material to help them with schoolwork. If parents don't have a computer at home, there are other places with Internet services they can access. The most popular place would be the local library, which can also be used to locate books that can help children with homework assignments.

What is really great about getting parents involved with their children's homework is the closeness the children will develop with their parents. Because of the extra time parents are spending with children, they will realize that education is important at an early age. Children love to do things with their parents, and if the parents are excited about education, then the children will also be excited. Parents should try to make sure children stay focused with the excitement that has been generated.

Sometimes parents can get so excited that they do the homework for their children. This should be discouraged. If parents start to do homework for children, the children will likely become too dependent on the parent. This will eventually hinder the children's development. Homework is for children—not parents.

As mentioned earlier, if children are not receiving enough homework from school, as a parent, there are additional things that can be done. Parents can go to the local bookstore and find workbooks that correlate to the lesson in school. Make sure you have a ready supply of extra lessons available for children. Also, if the children are in need of extra help in a subject, parents can utilize worksheets. Most Web site engines will display lessons in all subjects.

Another basic thing to do to support homework is to assign the children reading assignments at home that are related to the homework lesson. Parents should also keep in mind that these are young children, so don't assign too much extra homework.

Because of the extra time parents spend with children, sometimes they may feel as though they are attending school again. Parents should always remember the rewards the children will receive because their hard work will benefit their children for the rest of their lives. When the children have mastered a subject or a lesson, parents will know that all of the hard work does indeed pay off. So, parents, do not get discouraged.

Before children start doing homework, they should be taught how to tackle homework. Sometimes children receive homework from several classes on the same night, which could create some stress. In order to make this process easier, children should tackle the most difficult homework assignments first. Children will feel that everything is downhill from that point on, which could alleviate some of the stress associated with homework.

Children should also be taught to organize homework assignments, and not to wait until the last minute to complete those assignments. If a teacher assigns a book report or some kind of assignment two weeks in advance, parents should make sure the assignment is started well in advance of the due date. This is a perfect reason to keep a calendar and stay organized.

Extracurricular Activities

While raising successful children, many of the educational lessons will come from participation in activities outside of school. Children will get most of their formal education in school, but their education can be accelerated in some areas when exposed to extracurricular activities.

For example, if five-year-old children begin learning how to play the piano, parents will notice how quickly they develop other skills. Learning how to play the piano will enhance their reading, math, and listening skills. The five-year-old will demonstrate how to read music and how to count notes, which will definitely carry over to school. In addition to the skills mentioned, they will start playing recitals in front of crowds, which will give them more confidence at a young age.

Learning to play the piano will require a lot of practice, which is another important skill children will learn at a young age. Parents shouldn't forget the important role they play in this process by making sure the children meet all responsibilities and spend time practicing.

Another extracurricular activity young children may want to participate in to help accelerate additional skills is sports. Sports are important for a number of reasons. Children who participate in sports are developing skills that may not be learned in the classroom, but are important to growth.

After joining a sports team, one of the first skills children will develop is how to be dedicated to a goal. In society, people who are dedicated usually become successful in that area. In order for anyone to be successful on a sports team, they must show dedication by coming to practice and giving 100 percent each day. This invaluable skill can carry over to the classroom and life.

Another invaluable skill that participating in sports will develop is learning how to get along with teammates. This is an excellent way for children to learn how to get along with other children, which, in turn, will carry over to life.

Sports sometimes require children to be aggressive in order to compete. Some children are not aggressive and are really shy around other children. Sports may not erase shyness, but it will teach children how to compete in order to win. In this world, parents know that if people don't know how to compete, they run the risk of being left behind. The competitiveness that children develop when participating in sports is one the most valuable skills children can learn.

When parents watch television and see many former athletes that are now sports announcers, movie stars, or successful in other careers, they definitely can see how sports can carry over to other careers. Even though some of those stars were given a unique opportunity, they still had to compete to keep those jobs. One thing athletes know how to do is compete.

Some other important skills being developed for children participating in sports include: being on time for practice and games, showing some leadership potential on the team, and staying physically fit, which is a lifetime endeavor. Parents will have children developing skills which they will carry with them for the rest of their lives.

Involving children in extracurricular activities during their early years should include some kind of cultural activities. As a parent, it is important to be able to talk with children about cultural activities such as plays they have attended or been a part of. The children who participate in plays or attend plays will have exposure to new activities and information with their friends, which will increase their wisdom. Also the dedication and memorization of lines in a play is very educational, which will be beneficial to children.

Children are a product of what parents expose them to. The more exposure children receive, the better all around they become and the more knowledge they will gain. Children who grow up in an environment without extracurricular activities, without sports, without music

lessons, without after-school programs, without summer-school programs, without cultural programs are at a tremendous disadvantage
educationally. Parents should take into consideration that children
who have been exposed to extracurricular activities are more apt to
score higher on standardized tests.

Education for children will continue when parents take a couple
of days out of their busy schedule to take children to museums and
discuss various artifacts from all over the world. Children will learn a
lot about the history of different countries. The increase in vocabulary
will benefit children when taking standardized tests. Knowledge is
power. The children who participate in extracurricular activities will
definitely be more knowledgeable. Extra curricular activities for children can never be left out of any discussion of what is important in
the development of successful children.

High Expectations

We know how important parents are in raising successful children.
Parents must also know that clearly defined standards and high expectations are necessary to direct the successful path of their children.
In addition, children must know the consequences for not meeting
expectations.

Research has shown that there is a correlation between high parental expectations and school performance. Parents who set realistic
expectations of their children can expect higher performances on cog-
nitive tests (Scott-Jones, 1984). These high expectations carry over to
positive life situations for children.

Expectations can motivate children to excel. Parents should start
at an early age requiring their children to be responsible in life for
their actions. Doing the right thing is not optional. It's a must. The
parents' expectations should become a way of life for children.

If parents discuss college throughout their children's life and instill a belief that all of their children are going to college, when their children grow up, they will attend college. The seed must be planted at an early age, and it will blossom

Elementary children who are asked to give 100 percent and try to earn A's in their classes need to have a plan from their parents on how to reach those expectations. If children don't reach those expectations, parents should encourage children to do the best they can. Parents should also remember when setting high expectations that the skills of their children should be taken in consideration.

The expectations for children should be discussed frequently. When observing children's behavior, parents should be firm and fair. Some form of reinforcement should take place as well as regular and consistent feedback. Parents' focus should be centered on the progress of their children. Lastly, parents must believe their children can meet their standards and expectations

This is an example of how one father had very high expectations for his son: When his son was very young (two or three years old), he told his son he was going to be a doctor when he grew up. For the next several years, he told his son to always tell people whenever they asked him what he was going to be when he grew up. "Tell them a doctor." Whenever people came to visit, he would prompt his son and ask him to tell friends and relatives what he was going to do when he grew up. His son would proudly say, "I'm going to be a doctor."

During his senior year of high school, the son's counselor called him into the office and told him that his grades were not high enough to get into any of the top universities and he should drop that dream of becoming a doctor. The young man went home very depressed because all his life he had dreamed of becoming a doctor. When he arrived home, he told his father what had happened. His father looked him in the eyes and said, "Son, what did I tell you that your future career would be?" Once again, the son said, "doctor."

His father took charge of the situation and had his son apply to a smaller college for his undergraduate degree. His son excelled in undergrad school and was later accepted into one of the Ivy League medical schools. He later became a doctor and has been successful every since.

This is a perfect example of how parents who have high expectations for their children and provide the support necessary can direct their children to be productive people in society. Later, the doctor went back to his high school and found his high-school counselor and gave him a copy of his medical degree. Hopefully, the counselor also learned something from the experience. Never count someone out who has high expectations for himself or his life.

Educational Outings

Providing an academic environment at home is not the only way to raise successful children. Some education benefits can be derived from traveling and visiting different sections of the country. Locally, there are activities that are beneficial to children and parents should take full advantage of them.

For instance, children can go to the zoo, parks, and aquarium in most cities and learn about animals. Parents can spend time discussing the animals with their children and answering questions. Children can write reports about their favorite animals. Research can be done on animals to help children become familiar with animals. This is an excellent way for children to learn about animals.

Museums are a great activity for children and a good way to discuss natural history. Children love gathering information about dinosaurs. Having children read about dinosaurs can be a fun way to quiz them on that subject when going to the museum. Parents can purchase videos that feature animals and dinosaurs and discuss them with children. Some of the information discussed from the museum will be aligned with school lessons.

Children's museums have hands-on activities for children. Children can try different activities related to science. These museums are fun and will hold the interest of most children. When traveling throughout the country, parents can seek out historical sites and visit them. Children can then do follow-up reading when they get back home. These outing are fun and educational at the same time.

Children can take pictures and write fun reports about their travels. Trips to the Grand Canyon, Cape Canaveral in Florida or Mt. Rainier in Seattle, Washington, are excellent opportunities to learn about science. All of this information can be kept in a scrapbook or photo album. This is a perfect way to have children produce something she/he will be proud to share with other children or their teachers.

Locally, children can be taken to various places to explore their career choice. Field trips to law offices or courts may influence a career in law. Visiting engineering offices, car production, or steel plants may influence a career as an engineer. Lastly, going to talk to a doctor and observing what goes in that profession may influence a medical career choice. Parents should provide as many of these field trips as possible for elementary-age children. These are the years when children begin to develop their career choices.

Taking young children on a hike is an excellent way to promote interest in and knowledge about the animal and plant kingdom. If you are not inclined to take them on a hike, perhaps the children can join the Boy Scouts or Girl Scouts and have that experience. The nature hike could be a whole new experience for children. The variety of trees, animals, and plants can provide many educational opportunities for your child.

Reading and Writing Strategies

4

Reading is fundamental. So why can't everyone do it? Millions of children and adults don't know how to read, and that is truly unfortunate. Our society should take some of the blame, because not enough is being done to promote reading for all people, especially at early ages. Parents have the power to change the neglect in our society, and it is their obligation to do so. Supporting this reading initiative should start from home and continue at school. Hopefully, parents will use some of strategies in this book to start their children on this wonderful journey of reading.

Most children learn how to read at school with various reading methodologies. Some children learn how to read at home on their own or with the help of family members. No one method is guaranteed, but some have had success for years. The method used years ago involved using phonics to teach children how to read. This method identified letters of the alphabet and letter combinations that were associated with sounds. Children who use phonetics sound out words as a way of pronouncing the word. This method was successful for the majority of children.

Another method used "whole language," which was started in the eighties. This method was used as an alternative to the phonics technique. It teaches children to read the same way they speak. The emphasis is for children to look at words in a complete sentence and try to develop the meaning of the sentence from words that the children already know. Accuracy is not always important at this stage.

Lastly, some children learn how to read on their own at home. These children usually start looking at books or magazines of their choice and someone reads the article to them. After hearing the words several times, they begin to read. Or some children may pick up books or magazines and begin to read without any outside input. The magazines may have pictures and items of interest to the child. Children seem to learn how to read on their own when they feel comfortable with magazines or books. These children are comfortable in an environment that is conducive to reading.

My son, Ronnie, began to read at home by the time he reached age five. I brought him a very easy to read Dr. Seuss book and started reading to him every night. A few days later, he began to read with me. It wasn't long before he was able to read the book on his own. Memorizing the words and the story was his key to start reading. He was later able to read other books. When he started the reading program at school, he was well on his way to success.

This section will provide reading & writing strategies to assist children with successfully beginning to read and write. By no means should you force your children to do everything in this chapter. The objective is to have parents help with developing reading at a young age. The parents should choose what will benefit their children.

The earlier a parent begins this process, the better prepared the children will be for school. Parents can begin by reading to their children while they are still in the womb if they really want to get a jump on reading. All strategies are designed for parents to interact with their children, but parents must take the lead and make reading a high priority.

Beginning Reading

As part of the preparation for young children, parents should start by developing reading readiness skills. These skills will probably begin around the age of three or four. Some of the skills include learning one's ABCs. One strategy was mentioned earlier when the children have alphabets placed all over their bedroom. Another readiness skill is for children to recognize pictures of items. Parents can make this an everyday practice to point out pictures and tell children what those pictures describe, then later ask the children if they remember the pictures.

And yet another readiness skill for children is the recognition of some basic words. This skill can be accomplished in a number of ways. One way is the word wall that was mentioned earlier. Another way is to purchase word cards and review them with children or take a basic book and point out easy words children can learn. Make sure parents take the time to pronounce the words several times for the children and then have children pronounce the words.

Parents should remember that reading development begins when someone starts talking to children. Sounds are developed in the brain which will help them learn how to talk. Over a period of time, a small vocabulary is developed. So don't worry about talking too much to children because that is highly unlikely to happen.

Virtually all children display an interest in stories. One of the simplest, most powerful ways to develop fluency with language is to read stories to them. Children become more interested at the early ages when they can touch and play with some of the objects in the story. This is a way to make the book real for children so their interest will be enhanced. Sometimes parents should try to find some of the objects in the stories so the children can identify with the object visually. Once children have developed an interest in stories, it won't be long before they start to read. If children want to read along with you, please allow them to do so.

Reading can start as early as four years old for some children, but five to six years old is the normal age for children to begin reading. Working with them at home will give children a good start with the reading program used at the local school.

Some strategies are considered a must for parents. All parents should purchase books for their children (four years old is a good age) and don't forget to have their names inscribed inside the book. This is good way to show children how important books are. Children will be so proud of owning a book with their name inscribed. They may be inspired to start to read, or they may develop a fondness for books. We do know that children love to receive gifts, and this gift will be cherished for a long time.

When children acquire some basic reading skills, we devise other ways to get them to read more. Children love to stay up at night as long as they can. Use that as a way to get children to read more. Parents sometime allow children to stay up later when they are read-ing a story to them. Take this a step further and put a reading lamp next to the bed and allow them to stay up fifteen minutes later if he/she begins to read a book. If the children don't want to read, turn the lamp off at their normal bedtime. Most children would do anything to stay up a little longer.

Read to children at the same time every day. Sometimes it can build excitement for the children. This could develop into a family activity where the older children are reading to the younger children, or get the entire family to participate. Children love to participate in family activities, so why not make them happy with a family reading activity?

Purchase a few audio books. Play them at home for the children. This can be exciting for them and encourage reading as well as im-prove the children's vocabulary and listening skills. The idea is to have children hear as many different words as possible. If children don't know what the words mean, the parent should explain them. Another way to make this even more interesting is to play the tapes when taking trips in the car. Since an extended time will be spent in the car, why not utilize the time wisely?

Parents should build some reading time in the day for themselves. This is an excellent motivation for children. Children and parents can discuss and share the content of the books they are reading. This is a good way for parents to be involved with their children.

If children don't initially understand what has been read, ask them to reread it. If they still don't understand, the parent should assign a smaller portion or section to be read. Once the children can comprehend a smaller section, more can be added. This process may take time. Children learn at their own pace.

Another strategy is to encourage older children to read to younger siblings. This is a way to build confidence. After reading to the younger children, allow time for discussion, giving children practice at developing comprehension skills.

To help build children's vocabulary, parents can collect ten grade-appropriate vocabulary words a week. The children should be asked to find the definition and put the word in a sentence. To really make this interesting to the children, allow the children to find words. Ask them to locate words they don't know. Parents should always remember to include children in all reading strategies and they will be more effective.

Make an agreement with children to keep a book of their choice in their backpack. Allow them to choose a book for pleasure reading. Don't set any guidelines as to when the book must be read. Just recommend that reading during free time would be a good use of time. Parents may want to set up some kind of challenge with children: Who can finish reading a book first? How many books can you read in a week? Whatever is decided, remember that instilling the love of reading is the ultimate goal.

As children grow up, they tend to want to do what adults do.

Parents should sometimes accommodate children. Subscribing to a magazine in the child's name is one strategy. Children will be excited about receiving mail in their own name. The whole idea is to encourage reading. What better way to stimulate reading than to receive books or magazines addressed in the child's name?

Whenever given the opportunity, parents should encourage children to read. When at a restaurant, have children read the menu. When at a car wash or any place away from home, have children read the signs. Another good way to use this technique is when parents take a trip by car. Children can read signs all over the roadway. This can be a exciting way to improve vocabulary and reading. Children love to play games, so make a game out of this strategy.

A different family strategy would be to have each family member discuss a topic of their choice for one minute. The family can try and make it fun. The activity is a good opportunity to share opinions with family members as well as build on creativity, spontaneity, vocabulary, and listening skills.

Have children sign up for a library card as soon as possible. Once children have the card, parents should take children to the library on a regular basis. Allow children to spend at least an hour in the library each time and allow them to check several books out each time. Require children to return all the books before allowing them to check out any additional books. This strategy is the same when taking children to a bookstore to purchase books. They should read what they have before purchasing new books.

The older children should be spending more time reading. Regularly reading aloud to your child is still an outstanding way to successfully increase reading skills. Reading aloud should be done whenever and wherever possible. Read to your child at the doctor's office, when waiting on food at a restaurant, when riding in a car on a long trip, or when just sitting around the house.

My daughter's name is Jasmine. She had a different approach to reading than her brother. She did not teach herself to read at five. She started at a different pace than her older brother. As parents, we didn't spend as much time reading to Jasmine as we did with her older brother. That didn't stop us from raising a successful reader who is now a more committed reader than her brother. My daughter possesses a quality that separates her from others, and that is the desire to be successful. How did we develop that desire?

Some children have a inborn desire to succeed; others need motivation and guidance. All children can end up with the same desired result, which is excellence in reading. Jasmine, our daughter, was smart, but she was in need of that extra push to become successful. Having an older brother to model success helped to motivate her. Use a sibling to model success.

The goal has always been to build a love of reading for both children. If parents make reading important in their home, the children will believe it is important. Jasmine was the kind of daughter who loved to go places, so we took advantage of her desire to travel. It really didn't matter where we took her. This created perfect opportunities to take her to a bookstore and purchase books for her. We went to the bookstore on a number of occasions until she began to beg us to take her to the bookstore. This technique encouraged her to read a book every week and discuss it.

Also, our family constantly told her how intelligent she was and encouraged her to read as many books as possible. Some of the books were books she would be required to read at the next grade level. This motivated her because she believed she was reading what the older children were reading. Sometimes we gave rewards to her when she completed a certain number of books. This became important to her. She's doing quite well as a reader. Parents need to look at their children and determine what situation is best for them.

Spelling

While reading is very important, so is development of a vocabulary to enhance the reading. Children should be able to recognize a variety of words and be able to spell them and derive the meaning. Parents can play an important part in this process. When children are preparing for a spelling test, parents can help. Taking the words being used on the spelling test and giving children a pretest is a very simple task. This will give parents an idea of how many words children already know how to spell. The pretest should be a paper and pencil test. The words children can't spell should be pronounced and put in a sentence for practice. Encourage them to study the words.

The following method is excellent for learning how to spell a word.

- Look at the word and say it out loud three times.
- Use the word in a sentence
- Close your eyes and visualize the word, then spell it out loud two times
- Write the word down
- Repeat the steps if necessary.

After children have successfully spelled the words, ask your children to take a final test. This test should include using the words in a sentence. Children can study independently after this process is completed.

Practicing spelling is even more important now than in the past because of the technology we use that spells for us. Computers will correct spelling, so when children use computers to write papers, the spelling is automatically checked for them. Children should learn how to spell rather than allowing the computer to spell for them. The computer will do all of the work for the children which could stunt their spelling development. Also, spell-check on the computer will not correct a wrong word that is correctly spelled, like using "their" instead of "there."

Flash cards can also assist children with spelling. A very simple exercise parents can use at home starts with flash cards. Find about ten to fifteen words that are age-appropriate for children. Print one word on each index card. Place each card face down on a table. Ask children to turn each card over and read it quickly. Mix the cards up and have children try it again. Next, the parent should take the flash cards and pronounce each word and ask the child to spell the word. Make it more difficult by asking them to use the word in a sentence after spelling it. Repeat the exercise as often as needed for mastery of it.

Parents can utilize the strategies in this book to develop successful child readers, but at the end of the day, one of the primary ways for children to improve their vocabulary is through pleasure reading. Pleasure reading will improve vocabulary, reading comprehension skills, and critical thinking skills. Once children discover the pleasure of reading, a whole new world will open up to them. Parents won't have to battle with the child to read again.

Writing Strategies

If reading is the most important skill that children need to be successful in life, writing is a close second. Writing helps to develop several skills that compliment reading. Development of critical thinking skills, organizational skills, written communication skills, and problem solving and analytical skills are some of the many attributes associated with good writers.

Effective written skills are important for early academic development which leads to success and future employment. People must be able to convey complete, clear information in a succinct way to effectively communicate in this world. People who can effectively write their idea down on paper will have an advantage in school and in the world of work.

Many careers require excellence in two forms of communication: one is being able to verbally communicate an idea; the second, being able to express it on paper. If these two skills are perfected at an early age, children will have more career opportunities.

The life we live is based on the skills we develop. Development of excellent written skills will affect our level of success in life.

Development of Writing Skills

Writing is just as important as reading. Children must be able to express themselves on paper as well as orally. Children need to feel just as comfortable writing as reading. When writing, children's ideas should flow as if they were talking. Constant practice will help. Parents should make this another high priority as they did with reading.

One of the early means of written communication for children is through drawing. Encouraging young children to draw is the beginning of developing writing skills. This is a good way for children to develop hand-eye coordination and be creative at the same time.

Children can start some writing experiences by printing the alphabet and their name. Once children are comfortable printing their names, other words can be attempted. This practice should be repeated. Neatness should be stressed with young children. Workbooks are available to assist with this process. Practice should be done regularly. Once the children are comfortable with printing, cursive writing could start. Usually this takes place in the second grade, but could start earlier if the children are ready. The Web sites listed below have free worksheets for reading and writing exercises:

Free worksheets online:

www.rhlschool.com

www.beginningreading.com

www.teach-nology.com

www.child-reading-tips.com/

When developing an important skill such as writing, children should have all the tools necessary in the home. Parents should make available to children the following tools: pens, pencils, erasers, note-books, and paper.

Once the tools are available and children are older, the parent can start utilizing the in-home strategies for writing development. The first strategy that is easy for parents to implement can start by having children write letters and notes whenever appropriate. Whenever children need to respond to someone, they should be asked to respond in writing. At first, it may be a challenge for children, but as they practice, it will become easy for them.

There are many opportunities for children to write responses to people. The teacher would be a good person for children to start writing responses to. They could even send a letter to their teacher. After receiving the letter, the teacher could possibly encourage children to continue the practice. This strategy could be extended to coaches and other people in the children's life.

To continue with the practice of writing to people, children can make this a little more interesting by finding a pen pal to communicate with. This exercise will require the help of the parent. When looking for a pen pal, the parent needs to exercise caution. Parents should inspect what is being sent from the pen pal to see if it is appropriate.

In the society in which we live, parents must be careful when dealing with the unknown. The parent can start this process by going online to locate organizations that specialize in connecting pen pals. Once a pen pal is found, the children will probably be excited about writing to someone in a different country. This could lead to more writing, which is important.

Another strategy is to have children interview someone in the family. Start by having the children write out a list of questions to ask the family member. Once the questions have been formulated and written down, the children should set up a time to meet with the family member. Parents should make sure children have notebooks, pens, and pencils to conduct the interview. After the children have completed the interview, have them write the answers in complete sentences. Parents should collect the finished product. Once the children are comfortable with this exercise, it can be extended to interviewing people from different professions. Parents can decide how far they want to take this exercise.

A lot of the strategies for children include the family. This is important because children feel more comfortable interacting with family members. Once they gain confidence, writing will become easier at school.

Teachers often assign book reports. This can also be done at home. One of the advantages of the parents assigning a book report is that this can be assigned at anytime throughout the year. Since children have so much homework throughout the school year, parents may assign a book report during the summer or whenever the children are out of school for a long period of time.

Book reports are good for the children for a number of reasons: children are able to articulate their thoughts on paper, will learn how to draw conclusions and put them on paper, will learn how to identify characters and know what a plot is. These are only a few of the benefits of a book report.

When parents assign book reports to children, they can decide what kind of information should be written. Parent should take into consideration the age of the children. The older the children, the more information parents can request of them. A good way to get a short summary is to ask the children to write one paragraph about the book. This would be all the information the parent would need. The main objective of this exercise is to practice writing.

As children grow older, one of the main keys to good writing becomes "organization." Help them to identify what is to be written, have them explain what they want to write about, ask them the sequence of events, list key words and ideas, and then have them start writing.

Children should learn how to approach a topic, write at least four sentences to support their topic, and then finish the paper with a conclusion. If this procedure can be practiced and mastered, they will have a stronger foundation to begin writing.

These exercises will encourage children to write. Parents can explain to children that when writing, they need to visualize in their minds a writing plan. Tell them when they close their eyes, try to describe the picture and then write about it. When they have a topic, children should question the topic, such as why they want to write about it. The verbal descriptions will help them to develop thoughts to put on paper.

Remember that a rich language environment is a fertile foundation for good writing. Taking time at dinner, in the car, and bedtime are perfect opportunities to practice conversational skills. Parents should continue to talk with their children and discuss their interests and opinions. Whenever possible, parents should ask children to read, spell, and write.

The activities listed above are just a few writing activities that you can utilize for children. Parents can develop their own activities. Never force activities on children. If writing is encouraged at an early age, children could become writers and even develop a love of writing.

Summary of Reading and Writing Strategies for Children:

- Parents should place alphabets and words on the wall of their children's bedroom.

- Parents should purchase word cards for their children.

- Parents should take children to the book store and purchase books for them.

- Parents should start family reading activities in their home.

- Books and magazines should be visible in the home.

- Parents should purchase audio books that may be used on trips.

- Reading books should be placed in the children backpack everyday.

- Parents should subscribe to a magazine in their child's name.

- Parents should make sure their child's signs up for a library card.

- Parents should allow quiet time each day for the family to read.

- Everyone should encourage children to read as much as possible.

- Children should be allowed to develop writing skills by drawing pictures at a young age.

- Children should practice writing alphabets

- Children should practice writing letters and notes to different people.

- Parents should locate a reputable pen pal company so children can correspond with other children all over the world.

- Parents should have children develop and write out interviewing questions before interviewing family members and friends.

- Parents should assign book reports to children and have them write a one paragraph summary.

- If children are having trouble writing, parents can introduce the visualization technique.

- Everyone should encourage children to write as much as possible.

Once children discover the pleasure of reading, a whole new world will open up to them.

Mathematics Strategies

5

If there is an area of education which children seem to be afraid to tackle, it is math. For some reason, children get discouraged whenever they are asked to do math. In the past, it seemed that this problem impacted young girls more than young boys, but that is no longer true. Confidence in math is now impacting everyone. This problem can be rectified if parents get their children involved with math at a young age. Parents must be positive about their children's math potential even if the parents were not good in math. Hopefully, parents will utilize the strategies in this book to point their children in the right direction.

Developing a good foundation in addition, subtraction, multiplication, and division for children at a young age is very important. All future math classes are based on those four math computations. Helping children to understand those four math computations will build confidence, prepare children for the many math-related problems they will encounter in life, as well as open the door to a range of careers. Also, remember that children who are successful in math are generally successful in science.

Parents should make math fun for children in order to keep their interest strong. One of the biggest problems young people have with math is the erroneous belief that math is so hard, or not relevant, or that their parents were never good at math. That kind of mentality must change in order to develop successful children in math.

In my family, our son and daughter were always told that math was their best subject and we provided them with strategies to ensure they did well in the subject. As a result, I am proud to say they earned A's in their math classes. This success did not come from their parents' math skills, but it came from constant encouragement, good teachers, and excellent math strategies at home.

Parents should look for ways to reinforce math skills at home. Whenever possible, involve children in tasks that require adding, computing, measuring, estimating, building, problem solving, and reasoning.

At the younger ages, children should be able to correctly write numbers. Research shows that 25 percent of math problems come from children writing the wrong numbers on paper. Asking children to trace numbers and say numbers out loud with their eyes closed is very helpful for beginning math students.

In addition, playing games with numbers is helpful for math understanding. How far can children sequentially count? Ask children what number is before and after a particular number. This simple exercise can help children to begin to think about numbers and in what sequence they belong. Also, stores have numerous of games for children that involve numbers. The key is parents making sacrifices to purchase those games and spending time with children by playing the games.

Children love to play games which involve dice. These games require moving pieces across a board, which is an excellent way to develop counting skills. Playing dominoes is also a good game for math development.

Some strategies should utilize items around the house to help with math development. For instance, have children estimate the length of a household item. Then measure the item with a ruler or tape measure to get the correct length. Ask children to guess the distance across the length of a room, then measure the room. This can help children work on estimation skills as well as measurement skills.

A fun exercise involves purchasing 35 pieces of M&M candy and ask the children to distribute an equal number of the candy to five people. After distribution, ask the children how many pieces each person received. Change the number of people to seven and continue to distribute equal amounts of candy, and ask the same question—how many pieces of candy did each person receive? This is a good way to teach division and multiplication.

Parents should also begin to teach children the value of money. That skill can give children the foundation that will be needed for their entire life. One way to begin is by giving children a dollar to spend when they go to the store. Have them purchase something and get the correct change. Monitor to see it they are given the correct change. As children get more comfortable, give them more money to spend at the store. This can help with recognizing denominations of coins and improving their adding and subtraction skills.

In order to help children learn about collecting data, the following strategy can be utilized. Ask them to make a shopping list of groceries for a special event, such as Thanksgiving dinner. Help them write out the list and discuss the items needed. Also, have them write how much is needed of each item. Choose a special dish to cook for that dinner and make a list of the items needed. When children go to the grocery store, allow them to find each item and compare prices for each item.

Encourage the children to estimate some items. If potatoes are $1.59 a pound or 50 cents each, ask them which is cheaper. Show children how to use the scale to weigh potatoes. What parents should understand is children can learn these skills at a young age if someone takes the time to guide them.

Another activity at the grocery store includes using only a grocery scale. Explain to children that the fruits and vegetables are sold by weight, and that cost is generally charged by the pound. The scale is divided into smaller parts, or ounces, and it takes 16 ounces to make a pound.

This is another way to show children how math is intertwined in their everyday lives. Parents should gather some fruit and ask the children to weigh it. Then take some fruits and ask children to estimate the weight. Next, ask the children to pick up one pound of grapes, two pounds of pears, etc.

Ask children several questions when working with the scale. For example:

- Which fruit weighs the most, a plum or a grape?
- If the oranges are 29 cents a pound, how many pounds can you purchase if you have $2 to spend?
- If pears are 50 cents a pound, how many pears can you purchase for $1.50?

Sometimes watching TV can help with the development of children's math skills. For instance, if you watch football on television, here are some basic questions that can help children in grades 2–6 polish their math skills. Parents should know something about the sport of football for this exercise.

Addition

- Your team just gained 5 yards on the second down, no yards were gained on first down. How many more yards are needed for a first down? (First downs are 10 yards.)
- The quarterback just completed a 25-yard pass on the second down. The quarterback was on the 20-yard line. Where will the next down start.

- If your team starts at the 40-yard line of your goal line, how many first downs will it take to reach the end zone?
- Your team has scored two touchdowns, two extra points, and one field goal. The other team has scored three touchdowns and three extra points. What's the score?

Subtraction

- Your team is on the 40 yard line and receives a 10-yard penalty. Where is the ball placed?
- Your team is on the 50 yard line, and receives a 15-yard penalty for holding, and another 15-yard penalty for illegal conduct. Where is the ball placed?

Parents can utilize these questions to get children involved with math, or they can create their own questions. When the children are older, parents can develop more difficult questions. The whole idea is to get the children engaged with math in everyday situations. Parents can use programs on television to help with the development of math skills. Parents need to review educational programs that are produced on television. Whatever additional activities the parents decide to keep children involved in, remember to keep those activities fun.

As children grow older, more advanced strategies should be used. Teaching children about investing is very important. The stock market is a tool that is widely used by various groups in society. Take a few minutes and explain to children what shares of stock are. Children should understand what shares of a company are before children can participate in this exercise.

Here is a hypothetical situation. Parents should give their children one thousand dollars to invest in shares of stock for a company. The children should be allowed to choose the company of their choice.

The object is to see if the children can make money from their investments. Ask the children to research on the Internet any company they spend money on. At the end of each month, the children should review their investments. What was learned? What will be done differently next month? Children will learn a lot about money, investments, the value of a dollar, company successes and failures, and how important it is to research through exercises like this.

Because of the Internet, we can include our children in several activities in which we are involved. A lot of our shopping can be done on the Internet. When looking for something on the Internet, give children a dollar amount and how much to pay for a product. Tell the children to go online and find the best deal for the item. Children love to assist parents with activities. This activity is another way to correlate math with everyday life.

Parents have a household budget that is important to their everyday lives. Writing the budget down is important to organize bills and to make sure the budget is followed. Children can also start a budget. Children should keep track of all monies they receive and how they plan to spend it. The earlier children are responsible for their spending, the sooner they will understand the value of money.

Children will probably initially have a hard time sticking to a budget. Parents can modify the budget if necessary by placing a large portion of the budget under miscellaneous spending. This will allow children to still be children and spend their money on what pleases them. As they grow, less money should be placed in the miscellaneous area. The children's budget could include items such as: saving accounts, church, books, gifts, games, clothing, etc.

Parents can develop a little puzzle for the children that is fun. Ask them to go into your bedroom and locate your neckties. You have 18 neckties hanging up in your bedroom, 10 are black and eight are blue. If the child were to close his eyes and grab one tie, what is the probability that he would choose a black tie? Since 10 ties are black, the chances of grabbing a black one are 10 out of 18. The fraction could be set up as 10/18. If you divide 10 by 18, the percentage would be 55 percent, so the child would have a 55-percent chance of picking a black tie.

These exercises can be changed to whatever you believe is comfortable for children. The whole idea is to give them as many real-life situations as possible so math can have some practicality for children. This should make the pencil-and-paper assignments more understandable for them.

Mental Math

Math exercises used to stretch the brain are good for math development and should be encouraged for children. If children can recall the answer to a math question without writing it down, they will feel confident and be able to compute answers to math problems more quickly. Practicing these mental math exercises can be useful in encouraging mental math skills

A quick way to do mental math with children is to go to the checkout lane at a grocery store and have them estimate how much the total on the cash register will be. Also, ask children how much change you should receive if the bill was $15.95 and you had a $20-dollar bill. Every time you spend money at the grocery store, ask your children to pay the bill and make sure they receive the correct change. Teach them not to leave the cash register until the change has been counted and is correct.

Whenever the entire family goes out to a restaurant to eat, play a game with your children and challenge them to come up with the total amount of the bill without using pen or pencil. Answers should be calculated in the head. Whoever comes up with the answer first wins! Also, ask children to come up with the tip amount if the waitress were to receive 15 percent of the bill. This should also be computed in the head. Children will increase their mental math skills if these kinds of exercises are done on a regular basis. Of course, children should be familiar with percentages before they do this exercise.

The more practice the children receive with mental math problems, the sharper their skills will be. A good way to keep mental math going at all times is to ask children to figure out the answer to different math computations in their head. Quiz children daily on math problems that can be calculated in their heads. For example, how much is two plus two, how much is three plus three plus three, etc. The older the children, the harder the math questions become.

Ask children to practice their multiplication tables and then recite them back to you. This practice should be done on a regular basis This same process should be done with addition, subtraction, and division. Always encourage children to try their best and provide incentives for coming up with the correct answers.

After several weeks of practice, have some fun with children and ask them several math computations sequentially and reward them if they can get the right answers. Examples, what is 6x2, add 6, divide by 2, and subtract 3? The answer is 6. After several practice runs, children will become comfortable with multiple computation questions. Once children are excited about answering these multiple math questions, other math computations can be added, such as square roots. Children as young as seven years old have had success with this process.

Have high expectations for children and they will not let parents down. Generally, students who have developed mental math skills have become excellent math students throughout their formal education.

Summary of Mathematical Strategies for Children:

- Parents should make sure children are writing numbers correctly.

- Parents should ask younger children to practice counting every day.

- Parents should ask children to estimate the length of rooms and objects in their house.

- Children should play games that require math skills.

- Parents should teach their children the value of money by allowing them to purchase things in a store.

- Parents should allow children to develop a shopping list and go shopping.

- Parents should teach children how to use a weighing scale.

- Parents should explain to children how the stock market works.

- Parents should show children how to develop a budget for themselves.

- Parents should ask children to estimate how much money it will take to purchase items in a store or restaurant.

- Parents should allow children to use the computer to help them with their math skills.

- Parents should ask children math computation questions and require an answer without pencil and paper.

- Children should be encouraged to answer mental math questions whenever possible.

Parents should make math fun for children in order to keep their interest strong.

Bonus

6

How Parents Can Improve Their Children's Achievement Level In Thirty Days

The information provided in this chapter was developed to assist parents with improving their child's achievement level in a short period of time. There is no guarantee of how much improvement will occur, but if parents are truly committed to supporting their children, your child will gain some success. As with any program, the amount of time and effort put into it will determine the amount of success your child will reap.

This program has specified a thirty-day limit for completion, but if the child involved in the program is showing improvement, the parent can continue the strategies for a longer time. The parent may want to continue a portion of the program for another two weeks before allowing the child to take a break.

The strategies utilized are basic and can be administered by any parent. All that is needed is love, a sincere desire to help, and patience to make this program a success. The program does not replace any of the educational strategies being utilized at the child's school: it will only serve to support those efforts.

Because of the connection to reading in all subjects, our efforts will be primarily focused on reading in this program. In a future book, we may offer a program for math. We all know that reading is the foundation of education, and the better the child can read and comprehend, the more success they will have in the educational system.

Program

This program will be best suited for children who have an understanding of the fundamentals of reading. The child should know how to read, and in the third grade or higher in order to gain the most benefits from this program. If the child is younger and the parent believes he or she can benefit from this program, then by all means, use it.

Deciding when to begin this program is optional, but we recommend utilizing the summer months when most children are not as busy with schoolwork and they won't be overloaded with homework. Even if parents go on vacation, this program can be continued without stopping its progress. A parent's attention and involvement of any kind is always a bonus for the child.

This program is designed for the child to perform activities for six days a week for a minimum of four weeks. The amount of time spent on each session will depend on how well the child can read. The approximate time recommended for each session is one and a half to two hours a day.

Getting started with the program is as easy as can be. Finding a quiet spot in the house and turning off the television during this time are all that is needed. Next, parents need to find several reading books that are one grade level above the child's current grade. We recommend asking the child's teacher to recommend some of the book titles that would be required reading for the next school year. Those books would be good to use for this program.

In addition to the reading books, the children will need pencils, pens, writing cards, folders, note cards, a highlighter, and a dictionary. Lastly, the child will need a vocabulary workbook that can be purchased at a local bookstore. The workbook should be at the same grade level as the reading books—one grade ahead. The workbook should have word pronunciation diagrams and exercises that use the new words in sentences. A small incentive to maintain the child's interest is also good motivation.

Because the lengths of the books will vary, parents are initially asked to divide the book into four even sections. If the book is very long, dividing it into eight sections for study would be acceptable as well. Each section will be read by the child each day of the reading activities and have a follow-up assignment attached to it. Parents can divide the book by chapters or number of pages as long as there are at least four sections. In the activities listed below, we divided each assignment by sections of thirty pages, which is our recommendation for the reading length.

Day One

The procedure is the same for each book the child reads and should be carefully implemented. The selection of the book should come from the teacher's suggestions.

The child should include the name of book, author's name, and introduction to the book when reading.

The first thirty pages of the book should be read at the child's pace, and all reading should be done by the child throughout the program.

The child should highlight anything in the chapter he/she believes is important and/or write the ideas in the margin. This would be an acceptable and valuable study tool.

The child should write on a sheet of paper the name of any words he/she doesn't understand. The definition of the words should be looked up before continuing with the reading assignment.

A thorough summary should be written about what was read and placed in the child's folder

The last activity for today is to have the child explain to the parent what he or she read. If you have questions regarding what was read, this is a good time to ask.

These activities should be followed every day for the same time period with each book unless another activity is suggested.

Day Two

The child should read the next thirty pages of the first book at his/her own pace.

As a reminder, the child should highlight anything in the chapter he or she believes is important. If the child wants to write important facts in the margin, this would be an acceptable and valuable study tool.

The child should write on a sheet of paper the name of any words not understood. The definition of the words should be looked up before continuing with the reading assignment.

The last activity for today is to have the child explain in writing what he/she has read. Parents should make sure the child's explanation is written in complete sentences. If there are any questions the parents have about the reading, this is a good time to ask.

The parent should collect the one-page paper and the words the child didn't understand and place it in a folder for later.

Day Three

Today's activity will focus on the list of unfamiliar words previously written. If the child doesn't have at least twenty words on the list, the parent should add enough words to equal twenty. The parent can use the words from the reading book or the vocabulary workbook. Please remember that the words should be at the same level as the reading book.

This activity begins with the child taking all twenty words, looking them up, and writing the definition on paper. The child should then spend some time studying the definition for each word. We recommend about twenty to thirty minutes for this activity. One good practice is to have the child write each word and definition at least five times until the child becomes familiar with the word and definition.

The child should then write each word in two complete sentences. If the children needs help, the parent may assist but should not do the exercise for them.

Parents should now take all materials away from the child and give the children a spelling test to see if they can spell and pronounce each word correctly.

The next test should involve writing each word in an original sentence to check for understanding.

Parents should look over both tests and determine if any words were misspelled or used incorrectly in the sentences. If any are incorrect, continued study would be advised.

If the words seem to be too difficult for the child, the parents should ask the child to write the word five times and spell it out loud five times. Review the definition and be sure to ask the child if he/she can put the words in a sentence. Parents should continue working with the child until he/she is familiar with all words.

Parents should collect all material and place it in a folder for a later review.

Day Four

The next thirty pages of the book should be read at the child's pace and all reading should be done by the child throughout the program.

The child should highlight anything in the chapter he/she believes is important and/or write the ideas in the margin. This is a valuable and acceptable study tool.

The child should write on a sheet of paper the name of any words not understood. The definition of the words should be looked up before continuing with the reading assignment.

The last activity for today is to have the child explain in writing what he/she has read. Parents should make sure the child's explanation is written in complete sentences. If there are any questions the parents have about the reading, this is a good time to ask.

Day Five

The child should silently read the next thirty pages of the first book at his/her own pace.

As a reminder, the child should highlight anything in the chapter he or she believes is important. If the child wants to write important facts in the margin, this would be an acceptable and valuable study tool.

The child should highlight anything in the chapter he/she believes is important and/or write the ideas in the margin. This is a valuable and acceptable study tool.

The child should write on a sheet of paper the name of any words not understood. The definition of the words should be looked up before continuing with the reading assignment.

The last activity for today is to have the child explain in writing what he/she has read. Parents should make sure the child's explanation is written in complete sentences. If there are any questions the parents have about the reading, this is a good time to ask.

The parent should collect the one-page paper and the words the child didn't understand and put it in a folder for later.

Day Six

Today's lesson should begin with the list of new words the child has encountered while reading.

There should be at least 20 words on this list taken from the vocabulary workbook and at the same reading level as the book.

After looking up the definitions, the child should then spend some time studying the definitions. We recommend about twenty to thirty minutes.

Once the studying is completed, the child should put each word in a sentence and write it on the paper. Each new word should be written in two different sentences. If the child needs help, the parent may assist them, but the parent should not do the exercise for the child.

Parents should give the child a spelling test to see if he/she can spell each word correctly. Also, make sure the child can pronounce each word correctly.

The next test should involve writing each word in an original sentence to check for understanding.

If the words seem to be too difficult for the child, the parents can ask the child to write the word five times and spell it out loud five times. The definition should be given by the child and the word should be used correctly in a sentence. Parents should not go forward until the child is familiar with all words.

Parents should collect all material and place it in a folder for later.

Day Seven

The child should have completed reading the first book and have a basic understanding of the contents.

There should be at least 40 new words in his/her vocabulary. If anything in the first week needs to be repeated, the parent can make the decision at this time to do so.

The child needs to have all summary papers, words, the book, and definitions from the first week for a review. Give the child plenty of time to review the first week's material and put together a short oral presentation about the book. Since the child did so much work with the book during the first six days, this activity should not be too difficult.

The presentation is only for the parents. Try and encourage the child to be as creative as possible in the presentation.

Suggest that your child stand up straight and talk in a strong, confident voice. Recommend that the child not look at the note cards much doing the presentation.

When finished, the parent should congratulate the child for completing the first week and for doing a good job. Ask the child if there was anything in the first week with which he/she may need additional help.

Day Eight

Choose the second reading book for the next several lessons. Just as with book one, the second book is read silently as well.

This process should be done throughout this program. This requires the parent to have read the same thirty pages.

The child should include the name of book, author's name, and introduction to the book when reading. The first thirty pages of the book should be read at the child's pace, and all reading should be done by the child throughout the program.

The child should highlight anything in the chapter he/she believes is important, and/or write the ideas in the margin. This is a valuable and acceptable study tool.

The child should write on a sheet of paper the name of any words not understood. The definition of the words should be looked up before continuing with the reading assignment.

A thorough summary should be written about what was read and placed in the child's folder

The last activity for today is to have the child orally explain to the parent what was read today. If you have questions regarding what was read, this is a good time to ask.

Day Nine

The child should read the next thirty pages of the second book at his/her own pace.

As a reminder, the child should highlight anything in the chapter he or she believes is important. If the child wants to write important facts in the margin, this would be an acceptable and valuable study tool.

The child should write on a sheet of paper the name of any words not understood. The definition of the words should be looked up before continuing with the reading assignment.

The last activity for today is to have the child explain in writing what was read. Parents should make sure the child's explanation is written in complete sentences. If there are any questions the parents have about the reading, this is a good time to ask.

The parent should collect the one-page paper and the words the child didn't understand and place them in a folder for later.

Day Ten

Today's activity will focus on the list of unfamiliar words previously written. Please remember that the words should be at the same level as the reading book.

The definition for each word should be written. The child should then spend some time studying the definition for each word. We recommend about twenty to thirty minutes for this activity. One good practice is to have the child write each word and definition at least five times until the child becomes familiar with the word and definition.

Each word should be written in two original sentences to check for understanding.

Parents should now take all material away from the child and give the child a spelling test to see if he/she can spell and pronounce each word correctly.

The next test should involve writing each word in an original sentence to check for understanding.

If the words seem to be too difficult for the child, the parents should ask the child to write and spell it out loud five times. Review the definition and be sure to ask the child to put the words in a sentence. Parents should continue working with the child until he/she is familiar with all words.

Parents should collect all material and place it in a folder for a later review.

Day Eleven

The child should read the next thirty pages of the second book at his/her own pace. The same routine should be followed as in the previous lessons, and the child should highlight anything in the chapter he/she believes is important and/or write the ideas in the margin. This is a valuable and acceptable study tool.

The child should write on a sheet of paper the name of any words not understood. The definition of the words should be looked up before continuing with the reading assignment.

The last activity for today is to have the child explain in writing what he/she has read.

Day Twelve

The child should read the next thirty pages of the second book at his/her own pace.

As a reminder, the child should highlight anything in the chapter he or she believes is important. If the child wants to write important facts in the margin, this would be an acceptable and valuable study tool.

The child should highlight anything in the chapter he/she believes is important and/or write the ideas in the margin. This is a valuable and acceptable study tool.

The child should write on a sheet of paper the name of any words not understood. The definition of the words should be looked up before continuing with the reading assignment.

The last activity for today is to have the child explain in writing what he/she has read. Parents should make sure the child's explanation is written in complete sentences. If there are any questions the parents have about the reading, this is a good time to ask.

Day Thirteen

The child should silently read the next thirty pages of the book at his/her own pace.

The child should highlight anything in the chapter he/she believes is important and/or write the ideas in the margin. This is a valuable and acceptable study tool.

The child should write on a sheet of paper the name of any words not understood. The definition of the words should be looked up before continuing with the reading assignment.

The last activity for today is to have the child explain in writing what he/she has read. Parents should make sure the child's explanation is written in complete sentences. If there are any questions the parents have about the reading, this is a good time to ask.

The parent should collect the one-page paper and the words the child didn't understand and place them in a folder for later.

Day Fourteen

The child should have completed reading the second book and have a basic understanding of the contents.

The child should have at least 40 new words in his/her vocabulary. If anything in the week needs to be repeated, the parent can make the decision at this time to do so.

The child needs to have all summary papers, words, book, and definitions from the second week for a review. Give the child plenty of time to review the second week's material and put together a short oral presentation about the book. Since the child did so much work with the book during the previous six days, this activity should not be too difficult.

The presentation is only for the parents. Try and encourage the child to be as creative as possible in the presentation.

Suggest that your child stand up straight and talk in a strong, confident voice. Recommend that the child not look at the note cards much doing the presentation.

Each week the parents should notice an improvement in the

confidence of the child. The more practice the child has in giving presentations, the more confident he or she will feel. When finished, the parents should once again congratulate their child for completing the second week and for doing a good job. Ask the child if there was anything in the second week he/she may need additional help with.

The parents should also provide constructive advice about how the child can improve the presentation. Make sure the child talks in a clear and strong voice. Parents should recommend that child not look at note cards too much.

Midpoint

Parents should start to see some improvement in their child's confidence in reading, writing, and oral presentations. Each week the parents should be looking for additional improvements. Whenever possible, the parents should give the child praise for a job well done.

Also, this is a time for evaluation of the child. The parents should decide if the child can handle reading more pages each day. It is very important for the child to be able to understand the pages read. If the child needs to read the assignment more than once, allow him/her to do so. Once the child feels comfortable with reading, the rest of the activities will become easier.

Days Fifteen–Twenty-Seven

The procedure for the next two books that cover days 15–27 is the same as in the first seven days. Remember repetition, consistency, and persistence are necessary for good study habits and, as consequence, achievement to occur.

The last activity for today is to have the child explain to you, the parent, what was read today. Parents should make sure the child's explanation is in complete sentences. If parents have a question or would like to make comments on what was read, this is a good time to do so. Whatever the parent does, it must be done in a positive way. For example: "Son, you did a good job of explaining what was in the first two chapters of the book, but next time, it will be even better if you explain who the characters were in the book."

Day Twenty-Eight

Today is Family Presentation Day. Previously, the reports have been delivered in front of only one family member. At this time, and if the program has been followed as indicated, the student should be very comfortable with his/her achievements.

When the child is completely ready to give the presentation, ask the child to stand up in front of family and give the presentation. The family should sit about ten to fifteen feet away from child. Each week, the parents should have noticed an improvement in the child's confidence level. The more practice the child has in giving presentations, the more confident he or she will feel. Upon completion, the audience should once again congratulate the child for completing the fourth week and for doing a good job.

Make these last days important and encourage your child to keep up the good work. Perhaps even a special activity such as a dinner or picnic can be planned to show appreciation for a job well done.

Education must be celebrated and shown to be important to everyone concerned in order for your child to love it.

Twenty-Nine

The parent should find all 160 words with definitions from the past four weeks and ask the child to review all words.

This is the time the parent will need to put together a multiple choice test with all the words and definitions on it. The test should be administered to the child.

The parent should take a few minutes and score the test and give the results back to the child. If the score is above 90 percent, be sure to put a happy face on the paper.

If the score was low, the parent should review with the child the words that were marked wrong and have the child write those words and definitions five times on a sheet of paper. Also ask the child to use those words in a sentence. After completion of the activity, give the entire test to the child again. Repeat this process as much as possible.

After the test is completed, the parent should randomly choose words from the list and ask the child to put the words in a complete sentence and write it down on a sheet of paper. The parent should check the sentences for accuracy and make comments to child.

Day Thirty

This is the last day of this program, and the child should have a final exam on some of the information learned the last four weeks to see how much of the material was retained.

The parents should locate all summary papers for the last four weeks with all additional material utilized. With that material, the parent should develop about four to six questions for each book the child read. Make sure the questions come straight from the summary sheets. Do not try to trick the child.

Before administering the final test to the child, the parent should allow the child to review all summary sheets for as much time as needed. After the child has had time to review material, the parent should collect all material and distribute two blank sheets of paper. The final exam should be given to child in a quiet room.

The test should be graded and given back to the child. Hopefully, the child will answer all the questions correctly.

Always remember that your child can repeat anything in this program that was not understood.

Conclusion

This book can be very beneficial to the parents that don't mind getting involved with their children to make sure they have an opportunity to be successful at school and beyond. We have provided some basic strategies that parents can utilize to help improve children's achievement level. This book concentrates on improving reading, writing, and math skills. We have attempted to make the strategies easy to follow for children and parents.

This book should only be one of the many tools available for the parents to make sure their children are being prepared for the educational system. Thank you for reading this book, and may God bless both the parents and the children.

—Ronnie Phillips

Additional Resources for Parents

Tadlock, D. 2005. Read Right. McGraw-Hill.

Covey, S. 1998 The 7 Habits of Highly Effective Teens. A Fireside Book.

Chin, T. 2004. School Sense. Santa Monica Press.

Bates, L. 1985. Your Seven Year Old. Dell Publishing.

McCarney, S.1988. Pre-Referral Intervention Manual. Hawthorne Educational Services.

National Research Council. 1999. Starting Out Right. National Academy Press.

Bates, L. 1990. Nine Year Old. Dell Publishing.

Adams, M. 1994. Beginning To Read. The MIT Press.

Devantier, A. 2002. 101 Things Every Kid Should Do Growing Up. Sourcebooks,Inc.

Family Book & Wellness Guide Task Force of Oakland County. 1988. Family Fun Book.

Sears. W. 2002. The Successful Child. Little Brown and Company.

www.ceap.wsc.edu. Reading Strategies for Parents.

www.focusonyourchild.com. The Secret to Your Child's Academic Success, Teaching Your Child to Organize, Take Charge of Your Children's Education, Goal Setting With Your Children, Portfolio of Learning.

www.readingrockets.org. Reading Rockets: Is There Something I Could Buy That Would Help My Child To Read Better?

www.indianest.com. Reading Strategies, by Kamna Raj.

www.parenting.umn.edu. All Parents Are Teachers.

www.familyeducation.com. Top Ten Ways to Improve Reading Skills, Skill Kids Need to Read, Top Ten Ways to Help Your Kids Get A's, Eleven Tips to Help Your Child Prepare for Tests, Top Ten Homework Helpers for Helpless Parents.

www.childdevelopmentinfo.com. Improving Reading For Children and Teen.

www.search-institute.org. Forty Developmental Assets.

www.edu.gov.on.ca/eng/document. Helping Your Child Learn Math.

www.d21.k12.il.us. Doing Math at Home.

www.teacher.scholastic.com. 7 Basics for Teaching Arithmetic Today.

www.santarosa.edu. Being a Successful Student.

www.rci.rutgers.edu. Successful Students.

www.childcareaware.org. Family Routines and Rituals.

www.studysmart.net. Articles for Parents to Help Your Students Be More Successful in School.

www.succeedtoread.com. Teach a Child to Read—Phonics vs. Whole Language.

www.ncrel.org. Mental Math.

www.pbs.org. Basics of Math.

www.homepages.wmich.edu. Math Strategy.

www.urbanext.uiuc. Helping Children Succeed in School.

www.spring-ford.net. Comprehension Strategies.

CPSIA information can be obtained
at www.ICGtesting.com
Printed in the USA
LVOW13s0422010518
575465LV00002B/20/P

9 781432 743284